Journey to the Undersea Gardens

By Margaret Clyne, Rachel Griffiths, and Cynthia Benjamin

CELEBRATION PRESS

Pearson Learning Group

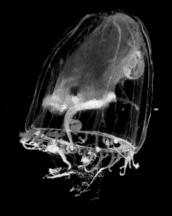

Contents

Introduction

This is the true story of a strange place called the Rose Garden. It is unlike any garden you've ever seen. This garden grew at the bottom of the Pacific Ocean. Scientists found the Rose Garden in 1979. They visited it again several times after that.

What is it like at the bottom of the deep ocean? People have asked this question for hundreds of years. Deep-sea **exploration** began many years before the Rose Garden was found. Discoveries like this help scientists understand how the Earth and oceans work.

Exploring the Seafloor

One early journey to the bottom of the ocean was in 1974. On this trip a team of French and American scientists explored the **seafloor** of the Atlantic Ocean. One purpose of the trip was to look for **hot springs**. These are places where very hot water flows up from deep underground.

The scientists knew that, on land, hot springs are found near volcanoes. There are also volcanoes on the seafloor. So the researchers thought there might be hot springs on the seafloor, too.

116 words

hot springs at Yellowstone National Park, Wyoming

Seafloor Hot Springs

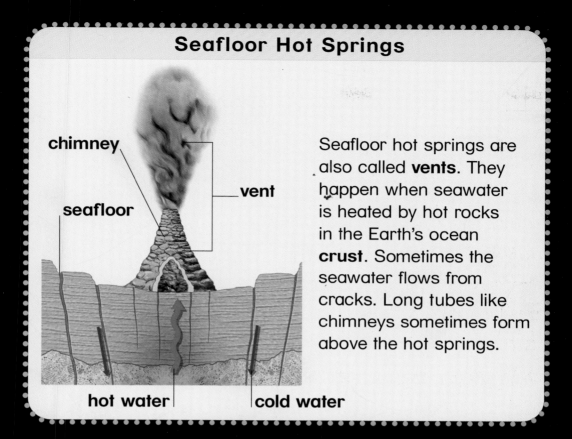

chimney

seafloor

vent

hot water

cold water

Seafloor hot springs are also called **vents**. They happen when seawater is heated by hot rocks in the Earth's ocean **crust**. Sometimes the seawater flows from cracks. Long tubes like chimneys sometimes form above the hot springs.

The scientists searched areas of the floor of the Atlantic Ocean in small submarines. They found some underwater volcanoes. The team saw **lava** rock all around the volcanoes. However, they did not find any hot springs. So scientists kept studying the ocean.

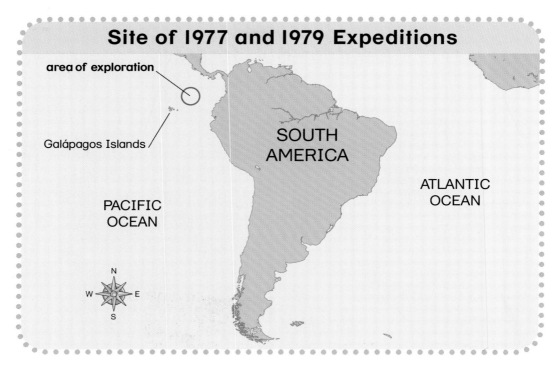

Site of 1977 and 1979 Expeditions

area of exploration

Galápagos Islands

SOUTH AMERICA

ATLANTIC OCEAN

PACIFIC OCEAN

N W E S

In 1977 researchers were working in the Pacific Ocean. They found an area of the seafloor where the temperature was cooler than it should have been. This was near the Galápagos Islands.

Scientists found hot springs in this area. After exploring the hot springs, they also thought the vents might be a clue to explain how seawater is heated in the Earth's crust. So in 1979 researchers decided to take another journey to the Pacific Ocean to learn more about the seafloor.

An Amazing Discovery

The expedition took place in February. The people on this trip were from the United States. The group traveled by ship to the area northeast of the Galápagos Islands.

The ship carried a small submarine onboard. The submarine is called *Alvin*. The group made several dives down to the bottom of the ocean in *Alvin*.

Alvin

Alvin is a submarine that holds three people. It has three portholes, or windows. The submarine also carries lights and cameras for taking pictures under water.

Alvin is launched into the water from the back of a ship.

Alvin travels slowly. It takes about two hours
for the submarine to reach the seafloor.

The crew had to travel down in *Alvin* for about
2 miles to reach the seafloor. The pilot steered *Alvin*
down to the bottom of the ocean. When the crew
looked out of the portholes, it was totally dark.
That is because there is no sunlight in these deep
parts of the ocean.

The crew had to use lights to see objects deep under the ocean. The lights allowed them to see out of the portholes. They saw many different kinds of fish and jellyfish on their dives.

On one dive the scientists saw the seafloor hot springs. However, that wasn't all they found. On the seafloor around the hot springs was the biggest surprise of all.

The scientists saw colorful jellyfish out of the portholes on their way down to the seafloor.

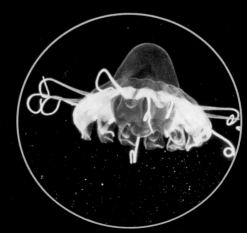

periphylla jellyfish

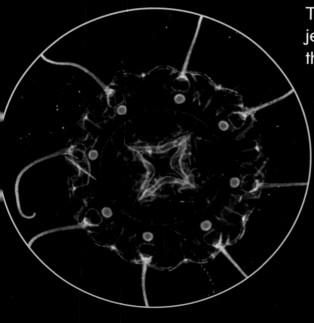

scyphomedusa jellyfish

The scientists were amazed to find clusters
of animals living close to the vents. The animals
were strange looking. Many had never been seen
before this trip. "We came upon a fabulous scene,"
said scientist John Edmond. "We saw reefs
of mussels and fields of giant clams."

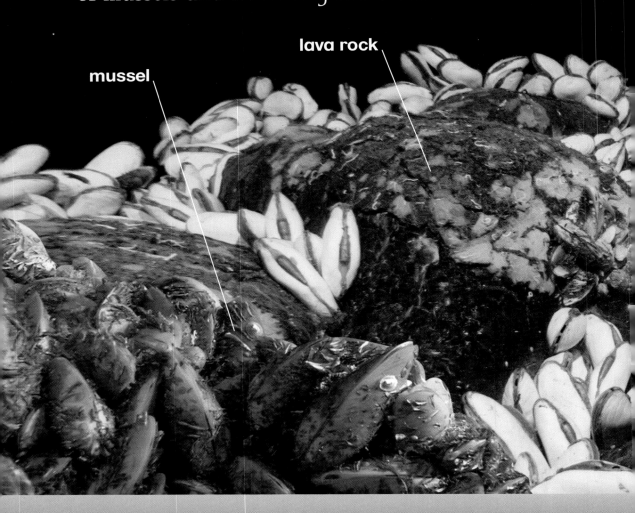

lava rock

mussel

One kind of animal that lives near the vent is a giant clam. These clams are more than a foot long. Perhaps the strangest animal is the tubeworm. It lives in a long, white tube that is red at the top. Tubeworms sway in the water like flowers in a gentle breeze.

giant clam

tubeworm

Tubeworms

Tubeworms are sea worms. They can grow to 8 feet long. They do not have mouths, eyes, or stomachs.

Chemicals from the underwater vents helped keep the animals alive.

Why were scientists surprised by this discovery? The animals found around the vent lived in a whole different way. They survived without sunlight!

Scientists discovered that something else kept the animals alive. They found **chemicals** in the hot water. The chemicals came out of the hot springs. The animals that lived around the vent were kept alive by chemicals in the water rather than sunlight.

The animals around the vent needed the chemicals to stay alive. Some of the smallest forms of life in the ocean used the chemicals to make food. The larger animals near the vent then ate the smaller life-forms and other small animals that lived off the vents.

Animals called spaghetti worms lived near the vents.

Tubeworms bloomed in the Rose Garden.

    Scientists named this amazing place Rose Garden because the tubeworms looked like roses. During the exploration water and rock samples were collected. Scientists also took many photographs. This information helped others study the Rose Garden more carefully.

At the end of their visit, the group left behind markers. They wanted to mark the places they had studied. This way other scientists knew where to return.

Over the years researchers returned to the undersea garden several times. They wanted to find out more about the animals. Each time they left more markers. Would people keep finding these markers in the future? On one trip they found the answer.

Markers helped scientists return to the Rose Garden.

Return to the Rose Garden

A new group of American scientists returned to the Rose Garden in 2002. They wanted to see how the animals had changed. They also wanted to look for new animals and make more detailed maps. There was still so much to learn about the vent community.

Scientists gathered onboard the ship *Atlantis* near the Galápagos Islands.

Alvin pilot Phil Forte and scientist Tim Shank worked inside *Alvin*.

The expedition began on May 24, 2002, and lasted twelve days. About fifty people worked together including scientists, the ship's crew, and **engineers**. *Alvin* was used again for the trip. The *Alvin* engineers made sure that the submarine was ready to explore the ocean floor.

Alvin moved across the ocean floor as the scientists looked for the Rose Garden. However, the markers were gone. What had happened to the Rose Garden?

Alvin was in the right place, but the crew inside couldn't see the Rose Garden. Instead they saw folded lava rock on the seafloor. Dan Fornari was one of the scientists on the trip. He said, "The Rose Garden may have been paved over by a fast-moving river of lava."

Lava rock was found on the ocean floor.

Young animals living around a new vent surprised scientists.

Then the crew in *Alvin* saw something exciting. They discovered a new undersea vent. This vent was in the new lava that had covered over the Rose Garden. A new group of young animals lived around this vent.

The research team thought that this new vent was recently formed because the lava was fresh. They also found very young clams and mussels in the area. Some of the tubeworms were only one inch long.

The scientists believed that this new vent was less than two years old. This was important because this new group of animals could be studied as it grew and changed. The scientists named this new area Rosebud. One day it might grow into another Rose Garden.

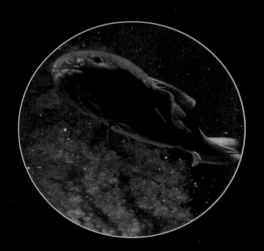

pink bythitid fish

alvinocarid shrimp

Young animals lived near the lava at Rosebud.

Alvin moved back and forth along the seafloor in the area. Many samples of animals, water, and rocks were collected. The scientists took many photographs of Rosebud.

Alvin's robot arm collected samples from the seafloor.

Now scientists are studying the animals and other samples from Rosebud. One day researchers will return to the undersea garden. What will they find? Maybe they will find more gardens or other unknown animals. They know there is more to discover beneath the ocean surface.

Scientists Tim Shank and Rhian Waller studied the clams that *Alvin* collected. ▶

Dan Fornari

Dan Fornari is an expert in using deep-sea vehicles to explore the seafloor. He is also a marine geologist. He went with Tim Shank and Steve Hammond on the expedition where they found Rosebud. Dan and Susan Humphris and Danielle Fino put together this Web site about exploring the seafloor: **http://www.divediscover.whoi.edu/**

Glossary

chemicals   kinds of matter or substances

crust   the outer layer of the Earth

engineers   people who use scientific knowledge to solve practical problems

exploration   the process of traveling to a region that is not known well in order to find out more about it

hot springs   places where very hot water flows up from deep underground

lava   hot, melted rock from deep inside the Earth; when lava cools, it hardens and becomes solid

seafloor   the bottom of the ocean

vents   openings or passages for gases or liquids to pass through